PRESENTATION

To _Diane_

From _Ron_

Date _Feb 14, 1974_

With all my love

From
This Day
Forward

Compiled by

Lillias M. Watt

THE WORLD PUBLISHING COMPANY
NEW YORK AND CLEVELAND

PUBLISHED BY THE WORLD PUBLISHING COMPANY
PUBLISHED SIMULTANEOUSLY IN CANADA
BY NELSON, FOSTER & SCOTT LTD.

FIRST PRINTING—1970

WORLD PUBLISHING

TIMES MIRROR
NEW YORK AND CLEVELAND

I take thee

. . .

To have and to hold,
From this day forward,
For better, for worse,
For richer, for poorer,
In sickness and in health,
To love and to cherish,
Till death us do part.

Spring

Live joyfully with the wife whom thou lovest all the days of the life of thy vanity, which he hath given thee under the sun.

Ecclesiastes 9:9

Love's Pledge

Entreat me not to leave thee, or to return from following after thee: for whither thou goest, I will go; and where thou lodgest, I will lodge: thy people shall be my people, and thy God my God.

Where thou diest will I die, and there will I be buried: The Lord do so to me, and more also, if ought but death part thee and me.

Book of Ruth, I:16–17

Wedding Eve

The wedding was to be in Fairfield [Pennsylvania], where the countryside was in its blossoming May greenness—so much nearer summer than Massachusetts, where the lilacs and apples trees would just be showing their buds! It was a strange, unreal time, those three or four days before the wedding—a time to me, as to most girls, I fancy, of misgivings. I was in love—oh, yes, certainly. But getting married? That was different—it was as final as dying, I thought.

I remember that the evening before the day, we wandered out to walk in the fragrant dusk by the river—the broad, brown, whispering Allegheny, on the bank of which were the woods and meadows of Fairfield and the big, hospitable house. We didn't talk very much, just walked silently, hand in hand, listening to the lisp of the river and watching the shadows deepen under the great trees along the path. Then Lorin said, suddenly, "Margaret, I would like to die, now, because I have touched the summit of Life!" . . . Of course we were only in the pleasant lowlands—the unseen "summit," which is Love, was still in the clouds! We couldn't know the meaning of the word until we had gone, together, not only through green pastures of Joy, but through valleys of Pain and Fear.

Margaret Deland

Solemnization

Dearly beloved, we are gathered here in the sight of God, and in the face of this company, to join together this Man and this Woman in holy Matrimony; which is an honorable estate, instituted of God, signifying unto us the mystical union that is betwixt Christ and His Church; which holy estate

Christ adorned and beautified with His presence and first miracle that He wrought in Cana of Galilee, and is commended of St. Paul to be honorable among all men: and therefore is not by any to be entered into unadvisedly or lightly; but reverently, discreetly, advisedly, soberly, and in the fear of God.

Book of Common Prayer

Of all actions of a man's life his marriage does least concern other people, yet of all actions of our life, 'tis most meddled with by other people.

John Selden

For G

All night under the moon
Plovers are flying
Over the dreaming meadows of silvery light,
Over the meadows of June
Flying and crying—
Wandering voices of love in the hush of night.

All night under the moon
Love, though we're lying
Quietly under the thatch, in the silvery light
Over the meadows of June
Together we're flying—
Rapturous voices of love in the hush of the night.

Wilfred Gibson

The First Flush of Married Happiness

We had a charming idyll here to-day. A young husband and wife came to stay with us in all the first flush of married happiness. One realized all day long that other people merely made a pleasant background for their love, and that for each there was but one real figure on the scene. This was borne witness to by a whole armoury of gentle looks, swift glances, silent gestures. They were both full to the brim of delicate laughter, of overbrimming wonder, of tranquil desire. And we all took part in their gracious happiness.

In the evening they sang and played to us, the wife being an accomplished pianist, the husband a fine singer. But though the glory of their art fell in rainbow showers on the audience, it was for each other that they sang and played. We sat in the dim light of a little panelled room, the lamps making a circle of light about the happy pair; seldom have I felt the revelation of personality more. The wife played to us a handful of beautiful things; but I noticed that she could not interpret the sadder and darker strains, into which the shadow and malady of a suffering spirit had passed; but into little tripping minuets full of laughter and light, and into melodies that spoke of a pure passion of sweetness and human delight, her soul passed, till the room felt as though flooded with the warmth of the sun. And he, too, sang with all his might some joyful and brave utterances, with the lusty pride of manhood; and in a gentler love-song too, that seemed to linger in a dream of delight by crystal streams, the sweet passion of the heart rose clear and true. But when he too essayed a song of sorrow and reluctant sadness, there was no spirit in it; it seemed to him, I suppose, so unlike life, and the joy of life,—so fantastic and unreal an outpouring of the heart.

We sat long in the panelled room, till it seemed all alive with soft dreams and radiant shapes, that floated in a golden air. All that was dark and difficult seemed cast out and exorcised. But it was all so sincere and contented a peace that the darker and more sombre shadows had no jealous awakenings; for the two were living to each other, not in a selfish seclusion, but as though they gave of their joy in handfuls to the whole world.

Arthur Christopher Benson

Mrs. Nathaniel Hawthorne to Her Mother

Concord, December 27, 1843

. . . We had a most enchanting time during Mary the cook's holiday sojourn in Boston. We remained in our bower undisturbed by mortal creature. Mr. Hawthorne took the new phasis of housekeeper, and, with that marvellous power of adaptation to circumstances that he possesses, made everything go easily and well. He rose betimes in the mornings, and kindled fires in the kitchen and breakfast-room, and by the time I came down, the tea-kettle boiled, and potatoes were baked and rice cooked, and my lord sat with a book, superintending. Just imagine that superb head peeping at the rice or examining the potatoes with the air and port of a monarch! And that *angelico riso* on his face, lifting him clean out of culinary scenes into the arc of the gods. It was a magnificent comedy to watch him, so ready and willing to do these things to save me an effort, and at the same time so superior to it all, and heroical in aspect—so unconsonant to what was about him. I have a new sense of his universal power from this novel phasis of his life. It seems as if there were no side of action to which he is not equal—at home among the stars, and, for my sake, patient and effective over a cooking-stove.

Our breakfast was late because we concluded to have only breakfast and dinner. After breakfast, I put the beloved study into very nice order, and, after establishing him in it, proceeded to make smooth all things below. When I had come to the end of my labors, my dear lord insisted on my sitting with him; so I sat by him and sewed, while he wrote, with now and then a little discourse; and this was very enchanting. At about one, we walked to the village; after three, we dined. On Christmas day we had a truly Paradisiacal dinner of preserved quince and apple, dates, and bread and cheese, and milk. The washing of dishes took place in the mornings; so we had our beautiful long evenings from four o'clock to ten.

Marriage resembles a pair of shears, so joined that they cannot be separated, often moving in opposite directions, yet always punishing anyone who comes between them.

Sydney Smith

Marriage is that relation between man and woman in which the independence is equal, the dependence is mutual, and the obligation reciprocal.

Louis K. Anspacher

To F. C.

Fast falls the snow, O lady mine,
Sprinkling the lawn with crystal fine,
But by the gods we won't repine
    While we're together,
We'll chat and rhyme and kiss and dine,
    Defying weather.

So we stir the fire and pour the wine,
And let those sea-green eyes divine
Pour their love-madness into mine:
  I don't care whether
'Tis snow or sun or rain or shine
  If we're together.

Mortimer Collins

Love Moves in on a Rainbow

It was raining outside their small apartment, and she felt nervous.

"I'm not kidding about the divorce—this time I really am going through with it," said Ella. "The way you acted at the party last night! What were you trying to celebrate so hard?"

"Never mind," said Tom. "If you want the divorce, I'll give you half my salary. What'll we do about the bank account?"

"There's only $12 left in it," replied Ella.

"O.K.," said Tom. "It's yours. Now what'll we do about the things in the apartment?"

Ella looked at him uncertainly for a moment, then said decisively:

"Let's divide them—since you're being so nice about the money. You choose first."

"O.K., I'll take your twin bed; it's more comfortable."

"Big man!" said Ella. "I'll take the other bed. Shall we divide the dressers —you take yours, I'll take mine? Right? Now it's your choice."

"I'll take the living room rug."

"That leaves me the bedroom rug. It's much smaller."

"I'll take the sofa and the floor lamp that works," said Tom.

"Big man!" said Ella icily. "I'll take the two living room chairs and the floor lamp that doesn't work."

"Good girl!" said Tom. "Just for that I'll take the desk and a broom and let you have the dinner table and the vacuum cleaner."

"How about the television set?" asked Ella.

"Well, how much do we still owe on it?"

"About $87—plus $12 repair bill."

"Honey, you take it," said Tom. "I want to be fair about this."

Then they got down to the things in the kitchen cabinet. He got the salt shaker and the cinnamon. She got the pepper shaker and the nutmeg.

Finally there was nothing left in the cabinet but a box of rice.

"You take it," said Ella. "You may need it to throw at your next wedding."

"No, I want to be completely fair about this," said Tom. Grain by grain, he methodically divided the rice into "his" and "her" piles, saying as he did so, "she loves me—she loves me not."

"Well, that was certainly a silly performance," said Ella, when he finished. "I guess that winds it up."

"No," said Tom. "There's one thing left—and I don't see how we can divide it."

"What do you mean?"

"Well, you were so upset when you came home from the doctor's yesterday that I went down to the corner and called him and he told me that he was pretty sure that—"

"I didn't want to tell you because he wasn't exactly certain—" said Ella, "and we both wanted this so much, and—"

"When I talked to him, he seemed pretty sure," said Tom.

"Is that what you were celebrating last night?" asked Ella.

"What else?"

Ella leaned over the table and pushed the two piles of rice together into one big pile. Then she walked to the window.

"Oh, Tom," she cried. "It's stopped raining. Come quick. Guess what I see!"

As he moved toward her in love, Tom didn't have to guess.

He could feel the rainbow coming in the room.

Hal Boyle

Washing the Dishes

When we on simple rations sup
How easy is the washing up!
But heavy feeding complicates
The task by soiling many plates.

And though I grant that I have prayed
That we might find a serving maid,
I'd scullion all my days, I think,
To see Her smile across the sink!

I wash, she wipes. In water hot
I souse each dish and pan and pot;
While Taffy mutters, purrs, and begs,
And rubs himself against my legs.

The man who never in his life
Has washed the dishes with his wife
Or polished up the silver plate—
He still is largely celibate.

One warning: there is certain ware
That must be handled with all care:
The Lord Himself will give you up
If you should drop a willow cup!

Christopher Morley

"I Will Make You Brooches"

I will make you brooches and toys for your delight.
Of bird-song at morning and star-shine at night.
I will make a palace fit for you and me
Of green days in forests and blue days at sea.

I will make my kitchen, and you shall keep your room,
Where white flows the river and bright blows the broom,
And you shall wash your linen and keep your body white
In rainfall at morning and dewfall at night.

And this shall be for music when no one else is near,
The fine song for singing, the rare song to hear!
That only I remember, that only you admire,
Of the broad road that stretches and the roadside fire.

Robert Louis Stevenson

Have you not heard
When a man marries, dies, or turns Hindoo
His best friends hear no more of him?

Percy Bysshe Shelley

Anthem

I knelt beside you in the darkened church,
And close to you I felt the wave of prayer
Wash over me like water cool and clear.
Before the organ played we heard it throb
As though God's heart was pulsing thru the air.
I looked at you and quickly turned away
Because your face was beautiful with prayer
Which only God was meant to see and love.

Forgive me if I have a woman's heart
And think of love at moments such as this
But when they brought the tapers like bright moths
To rest upon the candles cold and white
And touch them with a radiance of their own
I thought: So it has always been with us
You came and found me waiting in the dark
And touched me with the taper of your love
And now we glow together as one light
So calm, so sure, so beautiful to see!

And though I hear the mighty organ start
It cannot match the music in my heart!

Esther Wood

"That's the Girl for Me"

When I first saw my wife, she was thirteen years old, and I was within about a month of twenty-one. She was the daughter of a sergeant of artillery, and I was the sergeant major of a regiment of foot, both stationed in forts near the city of St. John, in the province of New Brunswick. I sat in the same room with her for about an hour, in company with others, and I made up my mind that she was the very girl for me. That I thought her beautiful is certain . . . but I saw in her what I deemed marks of that sobriety of conduct which . . . has been by far the greatest blessing of my life. It was now dead of winter, and, of course, the snow several feet deep on the ground, and the weather piercing cold. It was my habit, when I had done my mornings writing, to go out at break of day to take a walk on a hill at the foot of

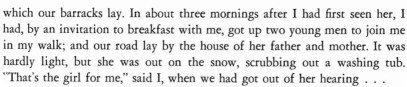

which our barracks lay. In about three mornings after I had first seen her, I had, by an invitation to breakfast with me, got up two young men to join me in my walk; and our road lay by the house of her father and mother. It was hardly light, but she was out on the snow, scrubbing out a washing tub. "That's the girl for me," said I, when we had got out of her hearing . . .

From the day that I first spoke to her, I never had a thought of her being the wife of any other man . . . I formed my resolution at once, to marry her as soon as we could get permission, and to get out of the army as soon as I could. So that this matter was at once settled as firmly as if written in the book of fate.

William Cobbett

Prayer at Evening's End

Here in this quiet room tonight
Where blooms a soft and lovely light
On tapering waxen stems of white;

Here in this room of hushed content,
Of love warm and beneficent,
Let me be mindful, we have spent

Some hours so good to live that we
Can face like kings the days to be!
Let me have vision now to see

The beauty of this thing we share!
The slow heart learns, to its despair,
No beauty waits for it to grow aware.

Adelaide Love

Summer

"She is my own,
And I as rich in having such a jewel
As twenty seas, if all their sands were pearls,
The water nectar, and the rocks pure gold."

William Shakespeare

The Blue Bowl

All day I did the little things,
The little things that do not show;
I brought the kindling for the fire
I set the candles in a row,
I filled a bowl with marigolds,
The shallow bowl you love the best—
And made the house a pleasant place
Where weariness may take its rest.

The hours sped on, my eager feet
Could not keep pace with my desire.
So much to do, so little time!
I could not let my body tire;
Yet, when the coming of the night
Blotted the garden from my sight,
And on the narrow, graveled walks
Between the guarding flower stalks
I heard your step; I was not through
With services I meant for you.

You came into the quiet room
That glowed enchanted with the bloom
Of yellow flame. I saw your face,
Illumined by the firelit space,
Slowly grow still and comforted—
"It's good to be at home," you said.

Blanche Bane Kuder

Antwerp, July 23, 1850

Dear Susan, I never see anything beautiful in nature or art, or hear heart-stirring music in the churches, the only place where music does stir my heart, without thinking of you, and wishing you could be by my side, if only for a moment. . . .

Your affectionate husband,

Wm. H. Prescott

What greater thing is there for two human souls than to feel that they are joined for life—to strengthen each other in all labor, to rest on each other in all sorrow, to minister to each other in all pain, to be one with each other in silent, unspeakable memories.

George Eliot

Things'll never run very smooth in a home where th' husband pulls out his watch in th' kitchen.

Kin Hubbard

A Cozy Heart

Once I thought that love
Was tempestuous,
Tumultuous,
"Kiss me quick."

I was wrong.

Love is usually a very comfortable way of life,
A cozy heart,
Kisses on the cheek,
"Wear your rubbers and blow your nose."

And what keeps a love so cozy?
The fact that every so often love is
Tempestuous, tumultuous . . .
"Kiss me quick."

Lois Wyse

From a Wife's Dairy

Nov. 19

Took out the last extra blankets this morning as the paper predicted "Fair and much colder tonight." Every once in a while the weather man is right.

"Such a remark is simply childish," says Jim.

"So is the weather," say I. Whereupon I slip another section of apple pie onto his plate and we both feel better. We agree on practically nothing —except the essentials. We two aren't one, by any stretch of the imagination, but we are two working together toward the same goal. The road seems a little foggy these days and the goal of happiness and security for ourselves and education and preparation for our children seems a mirage.

But, one day at a time, we'll accomplish it somehow. Nice to stand together at night as we cover up the children the last thing before we go to bed. Blankets he has worked hard to buy, and I have worked hard to care for, keep them warm and well. They are bathed and fed and made content because we have pulled together and made a success of our marriage. There comes over us both a feeling of peace and satisfaction.

Dorothy Blake

Sir Richard Steele to His Wife

I Love you better than the light of my Eyes, or the life-blood in my Heart but when I have let you know that, you are also to understand that neither my sight shall be so far enchanted, or my affection so much master of me as to make me forget our common Interest. To attend my business as I ought and improve my fortune it is necessary that my time and my Will should be under no direction but my own.

Distinguished beauty, brilliant talents, and the heroic qualities that play a more or less important part in the affairs of life, sink into a comparatively minor place among the elements of married happiness. Marriage brings every faculty and gift into play, but in degrees and proportions very different from public life or casual intercourse and relations. Power to soothe, to sympathize, to counsel, and to endure, are more important than the highest qualities of the hero or the saint. It is by these alone that the married life attains its full measure of perfection.

W. H. Lecky

Of all the home remedies, a good wife is the best.

Kin Hubbard

Love Poem

My clumsiest dear whose hands shipwreck vases,
At whose quick touch all glasses chip and ring,
Whose palms are bulls in china, burs in linen,
And have no cunning with any soft thing

Except all ill-at-ease fidgeting people:
The refugee uncertain at the door
You make at home; deftly you steady
The drunk clambering on his undulant floor.

Unpredictable dear, the taxi drivers' terror,
Shrinking from far headlights pale as a dime
Yet leaping before red apoplectic streetcars—
Misfit in any space. And never on time.

A wrench in clocks and the solar system.
        Only
With words and people and love you move at ease.
In traffic of wit expertly manoeuvre
And keep us, all devotion, at your knees.

Forgetting your coffee spreading on our flannel,
Your lipstick grinning on our coat,
So gayly in love's unbreakable heaven
Our souls on glory of spilt bourbon float.

Be with me, darling, early and late.
        Smash glasses—
I will study wry music for your sake.
For should your hands drop white and empty
All the toys of the world would break.

John Frederick Nims

In order to have a good spouse, you have to be one.

Love is the thing that enables a woman to sing while she mops the floor after her husband has walked across it in his barn boots.

My Wife and I

My wife and I, in one romantic cot,
The world forgetting, by the world forgot,
High as the gods upon Olympus dwell,
Pleased with the things we have, and pleased as well
To wait in hope for those which we have not.
She vows in ardour for a horse to trot;
I pledge my votive powers upon a yacht;
Which shall be first remembered, who can tell,—
    My wife or I?

Harvests of flowers o'er all our garden-plot,
She dreams; and I to enrich a darker spot,—
My unprovided cellar; both to swell
Our narrow cottage huge as a hotel,
That portly friends may come and share our lot—
    My wife and I.

Robert Louis Stevenson

Married life ain't so bad after you get so you can eat the things your wife
likes.

Kin Hubbard

I gave myself to Him—
And took Himself, for Pay,
The solemn contract of a Life
Was ratified this way—

         *   *   *   *

At least—'tis Mutual—Risk—
Some—found it—Mutual Gain—
Sweet Debt of Life—Each Night to owe—
Insolvent—every Noon—

Emily Dickinson

Bonnie Peg

As I came in by our gate end
    When day was waxin' weary,
O wha came tripping down the street,
    But bonnie Peg, my dearie!

Her air sae sweet, and shape complete,
    Wi' nae proportion wanting,
The Queen of Love did never more
    Wi' motion mair enchanting.

Wi' linked hands, we took the sands
    Adown yon winding river;
And, oh! that hour and broomy bower,
    Can I forget it ever?

Robert Burns

Marriage is popular because it combines the maximum of temptation with
the maximum of opportunity.

George Bernard Shaw

Be My Sweetheart

Sweetheart, be my sweetheart
    When birds are on the wing,
When bee and bud and babbling flood
    Bespeak the birth of spring,
Come, sweetheart, be my sweetheart,
    And wear this posy-ring!

Sweetheart, be my sweetheart
    In the mellow golden glow
Of earth aflush with the gracious blush
    Which the ripening fields foreshow;
Dear Sweetheart, be my sweetheart,
    As into the noon we go!

Eugene Field

A Prayer

I pray for you, and yet I do not frame
In words the thousand wishes of my heart.
It is a prayer only to speak your name,
To think of you when we are far apart.
God has not need of words. He hears our love,
And tho' my lips are mute, I bow my head,
And know he leans to listen from above,
And understand the things that are not said,
For love is prayer—and so prayers for you
Mount upward to Him eternally—
They are not many, and they are not few,
All are as one that ever seems to be.
     Thus do I pray for you, and cannot say
    When I begin, or when I cease, to pray.

Mary Dixon Thayer

That Day You Came

Such special sweetness was about
    That day God sent you here,
I knew the lavender was out,
    And it was mid of year.

Their common way the great winds blew,
    The ships sailed out to sea;
Yet ere that day was spent I knew
    Mine own had come to me.

As after song some snatch of tune
    Lurks still in grass or bough,
So, somewhat of the end o' June
    Lurks in each weather now.

The young year sets the buds astir,
    The old year strips the trees;
But ever in my lavender
    I hear the brawling bees.

Lizette Woodworth Reese

There's a bliss beyond all that the minstrel has told,
When two, that are link'd in one heavenly tie,
With heart never changing, and brow never cold,
Love on thro' all ills, and love on till they die.
One hour of a passion so sacred is worth
Whole ages of heartless and wandering bliss;
And oh! if there be an Elysium on earth,
It is this—it is this!

Thomas Moore

"A Little Lesson in REAL *Love"*

1854

Father doing as well as a philosopher can in a money-loving world.

In February Father came home. Paid his way, but no more. A dramatic scene when he arrived in the night. We were awaked by hearing the bell. Mother flew down, crying, "My husband!" We rushed after, and five white figures embraced the half-frozen wanderer who came in hungry, tired, cold, and disappointed, but smiling bravely and as serene as ever.

We fed and warmed and brooded over him, longing to ask if he had made any money; but not one did till little Mary said, after he had told all the pleasant things, "Well, did people pay you?"

Then, with a queer look, he opened his pocketbook and showed one dollar, saying with a smile that made our eyes fill, "Only that! My overcoat was stolen and I had to buy a shawl. Many promises were not kept, and traveling is costly; but I have opened the way, and another year shall do better."

I shall never forget how beautifully mother answered him, though the dear, hopeful soul had built much on his success; but with a beaming face she kissed him, saying, "I call that doing very well. Since you are safely home, dear, we don't ask anything more."

Anna and I choked down our tears, and took a little lesson in real love which we never forgot, nor the look that the tired man and the tender woman gave one another. It was half tragic and comic, for father was very dirty and sleepy, and mother in a big nightcap and funny old jacket.

Louisa May Alcott

Marriage: the Second Phase

. . . "Don't let us try to repeat life," he went on. "Don't let us make pretences to ourselves. Let us be thankful that there is an end of the old emotions and excitements. The excitement of searching is over for us; our quest is done, and happiness enough has fallen to our lot. Now we must stand aside and make room—for him, if you like," he said, pointing to the nurse who was carrying Vanya out and had stopped at the veranda door. "That's the truth, my dear one," he said, drawing down my head and kissing it, not a lover any longer but an old friend . . .

I looked at him, and suddenly my heart grew light; it seemed that the cause of my suffering had been removed like an aching nerve. Suddenly I realized clearly and calmly that the past feeling, like the past time itself, was gone beyond recall, and that it would be not only impossible but painful and uncomfortable to bring it back . . .

"Time for tea!" he said . . .

That day ended the romance of our marriage; the old feeling became a precious irrecoverable remembrance; but a new feeling of love for my children and the father of my children laid the foundations of a new life and a quite different happiness; and that life and happiness have lasted to the present time.

Leo Tolstoy

Fisherman

The earth has drunk the snow, and now are seen once more the blossoms of the plum tree.

The leaves of the willow are like new gold, and the lake seems a lake of silver.

Now is the time when the butterflies powdered with sulphur rest their velvety heads upon the hearts of the flowers.

The fisherman from his motionless boat, casts forth his nets, breaking the surface of the water.

He thinks of her who stays at home like the swallow in her nest, of her whom he will see soon again, when he brings her food, like the swallow's mate.

Stuart Merrill
(after Li-Tai-Pe)

My Life Is a Bowl

My life is a bowl which is mine to bring
　　With loveliness old and new.
So I fill its clay from stem to rim
　　With you, dear heart,
　　　　　With you.

My life is a pool which can only hold
　　One star and a glimpse of blue.
But the blue and the little lamp of gold
　　Are you, dear heart,
　　　　　Are you.

My life is a homing bird that flies
　　Through the starry dusk and dew
Home to the heaven of your true eyes,
　　Home, dear heart,
　　　　　To you.

　　　　　　　May Riley Smith

The men that women marry
And why they marry them, will always be
A marvel and a mystery to the world.

　　　　　Henry Wadsworth Longfellow

Thomas Hood When Looking Upon His Wife and Two Children Asleep

And has the earth lost its so spacious round,
The sky its blue circumference above,
That in this little chamber there is found
Both earth and heaven—my universe of love!
All that my God can give me, or remove,
Here sleeping, save myself, in mimic death.
Sweet that in this small compass I behove
To live their living and to breathe their breath!

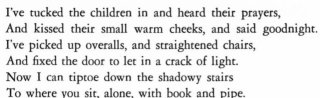

Evening

I've tucked the children in and heard their prayers,
And kissed their small warm cheeks, and said goodnight.
I've picked up overalls, and straightened chairs,
And fixed the door to let in a crack of light.
Now I can tiptoe down the shadowy stairs
To where you sit, alone, with book and pipe.

The kitchen's warm and still, and we two sit
In tired silence, for we need no speech;
I take the paper, look it through a bit,
Nor touch your hand that lies in easy reach.
So sure of love we need not speak of it,
Our hearts answer gently, each to each.

Nacella Young

The Memory of "Celestial Rapture"

Though the celestial rapture falling out of heaven seizes only upon those of
tender age, and although a beauty overpowering all analysis or comparison,
and putting us quite besides ourselves, we can seldom see after thirty years,
yet the remembrance of these visions outlasts all other remembrances, and
is a wreath of flowers on the oldest brows. . . . No man ever forgets the
visitations of that power to his heart and brain, which created all things
new; which was the dawn in him of music, poetry and art; which made the
face of nature radiant with purple light, the morning and the night varied
enchantments; when a single tone of one voice could make the heart beat,
and the most trivial circumstance associated with one form, is put in the
amber of memory.

Ralph Waldo Emerson

My wife is the kind of girl who'll not go anywhere without her mother, and
her mother will go anywhere.

John Barrymore

Love is a sweet dream, and marriage is the alarm clock.

Mr. Dooley said: "Whin we think we're makin' a gr-reat hit with the wurruld we don't know what our own wives think iv us."

Finley Peter Dunne

Sidney Lanier to His Wife

For I mostly have great pain when music, or any beauty, comes past my way, and thou art not by. Perhaps this is because music takes us out of prison, and I do not like to leave prison unless thou goest also.

For in the smile of love my life cometh to life, even as a flower under water gleameth only when the sun-ray striketh down thereon.

To His Wife on the Fourteenth Anniversary of Their Wedding-Day, With a Ring

"Thee, Mary, with this ring I wed,"
So, fourteen years ago, I said.
Behold another ring! "For what?"
To wed thee o'er again—why not?

With that first ring I married youth,
Grace, beauty, innocence, and truth;
Taste long admired, sense long revered
And all my Molly then appeared.

If she, by merit since disclosed,
Prove twice the woman I supposed,
I plead that double merit now,
To justify a double vow.

Here then, to-day,—with faith as sure,
With ardour as intense and pure,
As when amidst the rites divine
I took thy troth, and plighted mine,—
To thee, sweet girl, my second ring,
A token, and a pledge, I bring;
With this I wed, till death us part,
Thy riper virtues to my heart;
Those virtues which, before untried,
The wife has added to the bride—

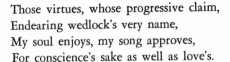

Those virtues, whose progressive claim,
Endearing wedlock's very name,
My soul enjoys, my song approves,
For conscience's sake as well as love's.

For why,—They show me every hour
Honor's high thought, affection's power,
Discretion's deed, sound judgment's sentence,
And teach me all things—but repentance.

Samuel Bishop

Earth Trembles Waiting

I wait for his foot fall,
    Eager, afraid,
Each evening hour
    When the lights fade . . .

I wait for his voice
    To speak low to me—
As a mariner lost
    Dreams of harbor, at sea . . .

I wait for his lips
    When the dusk falls.
Life holds my longing
    Behind dark walls.

I wait for his face—
    As after rain
Earth trembles waiting
    For the sun again . . .

Blanche Shoemaker Wagstaff

She would have made a splendid wife, for crying only made her eyes more
bright and tender.

O. Henry

She was a Phantom of delight
When first she gleamed upon my sight;
A lovely Apparition, set
To be a moment's ornament;
Her eyes as stars of Twilight fair;
Like Twilight's, too, her dusky hair;
But all things else about her drawn
From May-time and the cheerful Dawn;
A dancing Shape, an Image gay,
To haunt, to startle, and waylay.

I saw her upon nearer view,
A Spirit, yet a Woman too!
Her household motions light and free,
And steps of virgin-liberty;
A countenance in which did meet
Sweet records, promises as sweet;
A Creature not too bright or good
For human nature's daily food;
For transient sorrows, simple wiles,
Praise, blame, love, kisses, tears, and smiles.

And now I see with eye serene
The very pulse of the machine;
A Being breathing thoughtful breath,
A Traveller between life and death;
The reason firm, the temperate will,
Endurance, foresight, strength, and skill;
A perfect Woman, nobly planned,
To warn, to comfort, and command;
And yet a Spirit still, and bright
With something of angelic light.

Nathaniel Hawthorne to His Wife

DEAREST,— . . . Whenever I return to Salem, I feel how dark my life
would be without the light that you shed upon it,—how cold, without the
warmth of your love. Sitting in this chamber, where my youth wasted itself

in vain, I can partly estimate the change that has been wrought. It seems as if the better part of me had been born since then. I had walked those many years in darkness, and might so have walked through life, with only a dreamy notion that there was any light in the universe, if you had not kissed my eyelids and given me to see. . .

I am enduring my banishment here as best as I may; me-thinks all enormous sinners should be sent on pilgrimage to Salem. . .

But any place is strange and lonesome to me where you are not; and where you are, any place will be home.

Wedding Anniversary

This is the anniversary of the day
   Of days, for us, when we with faith and hope
Fared forth together; solemn and yet gay
   We faced the future, for life's upward slope
Was joyous going, and we never thought
   Then, that there might be worries—hours of pain.
And sleepless nights that left one overwrought—
   That loss would often come instead of gain.

But looking back, the time has not seemed long,
   Although the road, for us, was sometimes rough.
We have grown quiet and the buoyant song
   Once in our hearts sings low, and yet enough
Of loveliness still lives to make amend
   To us, for all the ills life chose to send.

Margaret E. Bruner

Anniversary

On the night of the twelfth of October, 1883, Henry George, who became famous as an economist and social reformer, wrote this note and put it by the bedside of his wife for her to find the next morning:

It is twenty-three years ago tonight since we first met, I only a month or two older than Harry, and you not much older than our Jen. For twenty-three years we have been closer to each other than to anyone else in the world, and I think we esteem each other more and love each other better than when we first began to love. You are now "fat, fair and forty," and to me the mature woman is handsomer and more lovable than the slip of a girl whom twenty-three years ago I met without knowing that my life was to be bound up with hers. We are not rich—so poor just now, in fact, that all I can give you on this anniversary is a little love-letter—but there is no one we can afford to envy, and in each other's love we have what no wealth could compensate for. And so let us go on, true and loving, trusting in Him to carry us farther who has brought us so far with so little to regret.

At Nightfall

I need so much the quiet of your love
    After the day's loud strife;
I need your calm all other things above
    After the stress of life.

I crave the haven that in your dear heart lies,
    After all toil is done;
I need the starshine of your heavenly eyes,
    After the day's great sun.

Charles Hanson Towne

Click o' The Latch

The silence holds for it, taut and true,
The young moon stays for it, wistful white;
Winds that whimpered the sunset through
    Sigh for it, low and light,—

Click o' the latch and he'll come home—
A stir in the dusk at the little gate.
Hush, my heart,—be still, my heart—
    Surely it's sweet to wait!

The tall skies lean for it, listening—
Never a star but lends an ear—
The passionate porch-flowers stoop and cling—
    Stilling their leaves to hear

Click o' the latch and him come home,—
A step on the flags, a snatch of song,
Hurry my heart, be swift, my heart,—
  How did we wait so long!

Nancy Byrd Turner

Quietly, Face to Face

I ask for a moment's indulgence to sit by thy side. The works that I have in hand I will finish afterwards.

Away from the sight of thy face my heart knows no rest nor respite, and my work becomes an endless toil in a shoreless sea of toil.

To-day the summer has come at my window with its sighs and murmurs; and the bees are plying their minstrelsy at the court of the flowering grove.

Now it is time to sit quiet, face to face with thee, and to sing dedication of life in this silent and overflowing leisure.

Rabindramath Tagore

The 5:32

She said, If tomorrow my world were torn in two,
Blacked out, dissolved, I think I would remember
(As if transfixed in unsurrendering amber)
This hour best of all the hours I knew:
When cars came backing into the shabby station,
Children scuffing the seats, and the women driving
With ribbons around their hair, and the trains arriving,
And the men getting off with tired but practiced motion.

Yes, I would remember my life like this, she said:
Autumn, the platform red with Virginia creeper,
And a man coming toward me, smiling, the evening paper
Under his arm, and his hat pushed back on his head,
And wood smoke lying like haze on the quiet town,
And dinner waiting, and the sun not yet gone down.

Phyllis McGinley

Accept dear girl, this little token,
  And if between the lines you seek,
  You'll find the love I've often spoken—
  The love my dying lips shall speak.

              *   *   *   *

You are as fair and sweet and tender,
  Dear brown-eyed little sweetheart mine,
As when, a callow youth and slender,
  I asked to be your Valentine.

What though these years of ours be fleeting?
  What though the years of youth be flown?
I'll mock old Tempus with repeating,
  "I love my love and her alone!"

                              Eugene Field

In the year that's come and gone, dear, we wove
      a tether
All of gracious words and thoughts, binding two
      together.
In the year that's coming on with its wealth of
      roses
We shall weave it stronger yet, ere the circle
      closes.
In the year that's come and gone, in the golden
      weather,
Sweet, my sweet, we swore to keep the watch of life
      together.
In the year that's coming on, rich in joy and
      sorrow,
We shall light our lamp, and wait life's mysterious
      morrow.

                      William Ernest Henley

Autumn

Love

To keep one sacred flame
  Through life unchilled, unmoved,
To love in wintry age, the same
  As first in youth we loved,
To feel that we adore
  Even to fond excess,
That though the heart would break with more,
  It could not live with less.

Thomas Moore

Love is enough: though the world be a-waning
And the woods have no voice but the voice of complaining.

William Morris

"Nothing—so it seems to me," said the stranger, "is more beautiful than the love that has weathered the storm of life. The sweet, tender blossom that flowers in the heart of the young—in hearts such as yours—that, too, is beautiful. The love of the young for the young, that is the beginning of life. But the love of the old for the old, that is the beginning of—of things longer."

Jerome K. Jerome

A Knight in Shining Armor

Fred is a New York linen salesman. He has never earned more than a small salary, but on this he and Clara have bought their home in New Jersey and have sent two boys through college. When I met him one day on Fifth Avenue he was shabbily dressed in a shiny old suit of blue serge—and you know how blue serge can shine. I asked him why he couldn't treat himself a little better, now that the house was paid for and both of the boys were doing well in their jobs.

"I'm carrying a lot of life insurance," Fred answered. "I've got to be awfully sure that Clara's all right when I'm gone."

He turned away, rather shamefacedly. A stray sunbeam fell across his shoulders and suddenly I saw, not shiny serge, but shining armor. Not Fifth Avenue, but Camelot, and a plumed knight with a sword at his side and his lady's colors worn across his coat of mail.

"What's the difference," I thought, "between that man and Lancelot? Those heroes of the lists fought twenty minutes for the woman they loved and Fred has fought forty years." There are millions of Freds all around us. Alexander's army marches into the subway every morning, gives battle, and comes back at night to millions of castles, where some woman has kept the little flag flying. That's why we continue to be a nation in spite of the grafters, and the gunmen, and the loose ladies.

Shining armor!

Channing Pollock

Debts

My debt to you, Beloved
Is one I cannot pay
In any coin of any realm
On any reckoning day;

For where is he shall figure
The debt, when all is said,
To one who makes me dream again
When all the dreams were dead?

Or where is the appraiser
Who shall the claim compute
Of one who makes you sing again
When all the songs were mute?

Jessie B. Rittenhouse

Mark Twain's Tribute to His Wife

In the beginning of February 1870 I was married to Miss Olivia L. Langdon, and I took up my residence in Buffalo, New York. Tomorrow [February 2, 1906] will be the thirty-sixth anniversary of our marriage. My wife passed from this life one year and eight months ago in Florence, Italy, after an unbroken illness of twenty-two months' duration.

I saw her first in the form of an ivory miniature in her brother Charley's stateroom in the steamer *Quaker City* in the Bay of Smyrna, in the summer of 1867, when she was in her twenty-second year. I saw her in the flesh for the first time in New York in the following December. She was slender and beautiful and girlish—and she was both girl and woman. She remained both girl and woman to the last day of her life. Under a grave and gentle exterior burned inextinguishable fires of sympathy, energy, devotion, enthusiasm and absolutely limitless affection. She was *always* frail in body and she lived upon her spirit, whose hopefulness and courage were indestructible.

"I mean," said Alice, "that one cannot help growing old."
"One can't, perhaps," said Humpty Dumpty, "but two can."

Lewis Carroll

To My Wife

Take, dear, my little sheaf of songs,
    For, old or new,
All that is good in them belongs
    Only to you;
And, singing as when all was young,
    They will recall
Those others, lived but left unsung,
    The best of all.

William Ernest Henley

Up and Down the Lanes of Love

Up and down the lanes of love
With the bright blue skies above,
And the grass beneath our feet,
Oh, so green and Oh, so sweet!
There we wandered, boy and girl,
Sun-kissed was each golden curl;
Hand in hand we used to stray,
Hide-and-seek we used to play;
Just a pair of kids were we,
Laughing, loving, trouble free.

Up and down the lanes of love
With the same blue skies above,
Next we wandered, bride and groom,
With the roses all in bloom;
Arm in arm we strolled along,
Life was then a merry song,
Laughing, dancing as we went,
Lovers, cheerful and content;
No one else, we thought, could be
Quite so happy as were we.

Up and down the lanes of love,
Dark and gray the skies above;
Hushed the song-birds' merry tune,

Withered every rose of June.
Grief was ours to bear that day,
All our smiles had passed away;
Sorrow we must bear together,
Love must have its rainy weather,
Keeping still our faith in God,
As the lanes of love we trod.

Up and down the lanes of love,
Still the skies are bright above.
Feeble now we go our way,
Time has turned our hair to gray;
Rain and sunshine, joy and woe,
Both of us have come to know.
All of life's experience
Has been given us to sense;
Still our hearts keep perfect tune
As they did in days of June.

Edgar A. Guest

Silver Threads among the Gold

Darling, I am growing old,
Silver threads among the gold,
Shine upon my brow today,
Life is fading fast away;
But, my darling, you will be
Always young and fair to me.
Yes! my darling, you will be
Always young and fair to me.

Chorus:

    Darling, I am growing old,
    Silver threads among the gold,
    Shine upon my brow today;
    Life is fading fast away.

Eben E. Rexford

My own dear Husband,—If I should depart this life before you, leave orders that we may be buried in the same grave at whatever distance you may die from England. And now God bless you, my kindest, dearest! You have been a perfect husband to me. Be put by my side in the same grave. And now, farewell, my dear Dizzy. Do not live alone, dearest. Some one I earnestly hope you may find as attached to you as your own devoted

Mary Anne

Mrs. Benjamin Disraeli
(Found among her papers
after her death)

Sympathy, the Perfect Love

When Love and Life first meet, a radiant thing is born, without a shade. When the roads begin to roughen, when the shades begin to darken, when the days are hard, and the nights cold and long—then it begins to change. Love and Life *will* not see it, *will* not know it—till one day they start up suddenly, crying, "O God! O God! we have lost it! Where is it?" They do not understand that they could not carry the laughing thing unchanged into the desert, and the frost and the snow. They do not know that what walks beside them still is Joy grown older. The grave, sweet, tender thing—warm in the coldest snows, brave in the dreariest deserts—its name is Sympathy; it is the Perfect Love.

Oliver Schreiner

Love New and Old

And were they not the happy days
   When Love and I were young,
When earth was robed in heavenly light,
   And all creation sung?
When gazing in my true love's face,
   Through greenwood alleys lone,
I guessed the secrets of her heart,
   By whispers of mine own.

And are they not the happy days
  When Love and I are old,
And silver evening has replaced
  A morn and noon of gold?
Love stood alone mid youthful joy,
  But now by sorrow tried,
It sits and calmly looks to heaven
  With angels at its side.

Charles Mackay

Tribute to His Wife's Beauty

She is handsome, but it is beauty not rising chiefly from features, complexion, or shape. It is not by these she touches the heart. It is all that sweetness of temper, benevolence, innocence, and sensibility which a face can express, that forms real beauty. Surface beauty is little more than the equivalent of cosmetics. Real beauty is spiritual. It is the only kind which is lasting. It is attainable through soul-culture.

Edmund Burke

A Golden Wedding

Your Golden Wedding!—fifty years
Of comradeship, through smiles and tears!—
Through summer sun, and winter sleet,
You walked the ways with willing feet;
For, journeying together thus,
Each path held something glorious.
No winter wind could blow so chill
But found you even warmer still
In fervor of affection—blest
In knowing all was for the best;
And so, content, you faced the storm
And fared on, smiling, arm-in-arm.

James Whitcomb Riley

ACKNOWLEDGMENTS

Grateful acknowledgment is made to the following authors, publishers, copyright owners and agents for permission to include the material indicated below:

ASSOCIATED PRESS, for Hal Boyle's column "Love Moves in on a Rainbow," *N.Y. World-Telegram,* October 11, 1961.
MARGARET E. BRUNER, for "Wedding Anniversary" from her book *Be Slow to Falter,* Kaleidograph Press, Dallas, Texas.
DODD, MEAD AND CO., INC., from *The Passing of the Third Floor Back,* by Jerome K. Jerome.
E. P. DUTTON AND CO, INC., from *The Thread of Gold,* by Arthur C. Benson, Copyright 1907 by E. P. Dutton and Co., Inc., publishers.
MRS. M. FREMONT-SMITH, for "A Prayer" by Mary Dixon Thayer.
HARPER AND ROW, PUBLISHERS, INC., from Margaret Deland's *Golden Yesterdays,* Copyright 1940, 1941 by Margaret Deland; from *Mark Twain's Autobiography,* Copyright 1924 by Harper and Row.
HOUGHTON MIFFLIN CO., for "Debts" from *The Door of Dreams* by Jessie B. Rittenhouse.
J. B. LIPPINCOTT CO., for "Washing the Dishes" from the book *Poems* by Christopher Morley, copyright 1929, ©, 1957, by Christopher Morley.
THE MACMILLAN CO., from Rabindranath Tagore's *Gitanjali.*
MACMILLAN AND CO. LTD, and THE TRUSTEES OF THE TAGORE ESTATE, from Rabindranath Tagore's *Gitanjali;* and for "For G" from *Collected Poems by* Wilfred Gibson.
WILLIAM MORROW AND CO. INC., for "Love Poem" from *The Iron Pastoral* by John Frederick Nims, published by William Sloane Associates,